THE BIBLE AND THE ARTS

Study by Alicia Davis Porterfield
Commentary by Judson Edwards

Free downloadable Teaching Guide for this study available at
NextSunday.com/teachingguides

NextSunday Resources
6316 Peake Road
Macon, Georgia 31210-3960
1-800-747-3016
©2013 by NextSunday Resources
All rights reserved.

TABLE OF CONTENTS

The Bible and the Arts

How to Use This Study

NextSunday Resources Adult Bible Studies are designed to help adults study Scripture seriously within the context of the larger Christian tradition and, through that process, find their faith renewed, challenged, and strengthened. We study the Scriptures because we believe they affect our current lives in important ways. Each study contains the following three components:

Study Guide

Each study guide lesson is arranged in four movements:

Reflecting recalls a contemporary story, anecdote, example, or illustration to help us anticipate the session's relevance in our lives.

Studying is centered on giving the biblical material in-depth attention while often surrounding it with helpful insights from theology, ethics, church history, and other areas.

Understanding helps us find relevant connections between our lives and the biblical message.

What About Me? provides brief statements that help unite life issues with the meaning of the biblical text.

Commentary

Each study guide lesson is accompanied by an additional, in-depth commentary on the biblical material. Written by a different author than the study guide, each commentary gives the opportunity for learners to approach the Scripture text from a separate but complementary viewpoint.

Teaching Guide

In addition to the provided study guide and commentary, *NextSunday Resources* also provides a *free* downloadable teaching guide, available at NextSunday.com. Each teaching guide gives the teacher tools for focusing on the content of each study guide lesson through additional commentary and Bible background information. Through teacher helps and teaching options, each teaching guide also provides substance for variety and choice in the preparation of each lesson.

NextSunday
Resources

STUDY INTRODUCTION

For many centuries, visual art, music, literary arts, and drama were closely linked with the people of God. Consider that paintings and sculptures of biblical characters and events are featured in most art museums and play an essential role in art history. Some of the most famous pieces of music are religious, even directly quoting Scripture. Handel's *Messiah* is just one example. Authors from Mark Twain to William Blake to Flannery O'Connor have religious themes in their work. Many dramas, especially medieval plays, depict the lives of saints and biblical figures. Decades ago, *Jesus Christ Superstar* and *Godspell* were huge stage hits.

Moreover, the Bible itself addresses creative expression. The tabernacle, a work of art made up of hundreds of smaller pieces, was designed by God and crafted by inspired humans. Our first session looks at the tabernacle and the artisans God called to built it in Exodus 31:1-11. Musical arts play a large role in Scripture as well, as evidenced by the Psalms. Young David began his court life as a lyre-player asked to soothe a tormented King Saul (1 Sam 16:14-23). The Bible itself is the word of God and contains hundreds of stories. In our third lesson, we recall Nathan's use of story to confront King David in 2 Samuel 12:1-9. The Bible also considers the use of dramatic arts in acting out a message from God—a kind of "performance art." Ezekiel uses drama and symbol in Ezekiel 37:15-28 to restore hope and imagination to the devastated exiles.

God has used artistic expression throughout the centuries to convey truth, offer blessing, and urge believers to deeper faithfulness. In modern life, artistic expression flourishes, from movies to books to music to paintings and photographs. Sometimes artists are intentional about trying to portray God's truths. Other times, perhaps God is working even when the artist is unaware of it. As believers, we may hear and see God at work in many art forms.

1

VISUAL ARTS

Exodus 31:1-11

Central Question

How can viewing and creating works of art bring me closer
to God?

Scripture

Exodus 31:1-11 1 The LORD spoke to Moses: 2 See, I have
called by name Bezalel son of Uri son of Hur, of the tribe of Judah:
3 and I have filled him with divine spirit, with ability, intelligence,
and knowledge in every kind of craft, 4 to devise artistic designs,
to work in gold, silver, and bronze, 5 in cutting stones for setting,
and in carving wood, in every kind of craft. 6 Moreover, I have
appointed with him Oholiab son of Ahisamach, of the tribe of
Dan; and I have given skill to all the skillful, so that they may make
all that I have commanded you: 7 the tent of meeting, and the
ark of the covenant, and the mercy seat that is on it, and all the
furnishings of the tent, 8 the table and its utensils, and the pure
lampstand with all its utensils, and the altar of incense, 9 and the
altar of burnt offering with all its utensils, and the basin with its
stand, 10 and the finely worked vestments, the holy vestments
for the priest Aaron and the vestments of his sons, for their service
as priests, 11 and the anointing oil and the fragrant incense for
the holy place. They shall do just as I have commanded you.

Reflecting

When you think of "art," what comes to mind? Welcoming
visions of life captured on canvas, in marble, or in wood?
Galleries full of educated people debating some new art theory

Leonardo da Vinci, *The Last Supper* (1495–1498)

that most folks can't even spell? Maybe you remember an art appreciation class in college, the one you had to take to fill an elective. Or perhaps you imagine your grandfather's woodcarvings or your mother's quilts.

These days, art means different things to different people. But for a long time in Western civilization, religion and art went hand in hand. Think of Leonardo da Vinci's masterpiece *The Last Supper*, Michelangelo's Sistine Chapel ceiling, or countless paintings of Jesus' nativity and crucifixion. Art was often viewed as a way to deepen religious devotion and education. Originally, stained-glass windows in churches taught uneducated believers the stories of the Bible and the saints.

With the Reformation, Protestant churches became less ornate than their Catholic counterparts. Icons "belonged" to the Orthodox Church; statues belonged to the Catholic Church. Yet even in the simplest country church, a wooden cross is commonly displayed. Its stark lines and rough edges speak a testimony to Christ's sacrifice. Many people would call that simple cross a work of art and declare the well-callused hands that carved it the hands of an artist.

When God gave Moses a vision of the tabernacle, every table, every carving, and every fabric was shown in vivid detail. God personally appointed the head artisan and his assistant to oversee construction. The tabernacle itself is a work of art composed of dozens of individual works of art. All of them are a mere reflection of God's glory.

> Do you think some modern-day churches have gone too far in restricting the use of visual arts in their sanctuaries? Why or why not?

Studying

For 300 years, Israelites worshiped in a movable sanctuary, the tabernacle. After giving the Ten Commandments on Mount Sinai, God instructed Moses to build a place for the people to worship. They lived in the wilderness, so the sanctuary needed to be mobile. It would house the presence of God and move as the people moved until they settled in the promised land.

Moses spent "forty days and forty nights" on Mount Sinai. There he sealed the covenant between God and the people of Israel. On the mountain God introduced the idea of the tabernacle. God commanded the people to give an offering for the construction of their new mobile sanctuary. It was an ancient building campaign! Unlike a modern church campaign, the offering came before the building plans had even been drawn up or approved. God chaired this committee of one and commanded the people to give everything from spices to yarns to precious metals (25:1-9).

With the donations and materials in hand, God gave Moses *seven chapters* of building instructions. Every detail mattered, from the exact measurements of the rooms and furnishings to the kinds of oil used at the offering table and fabrics used for the hangings. God gave Moses both a vision and detailed verbal explanations of what God wanted (25:40).

The detail of the artistry mattered so much because every surface, every stitch, and every aroma would reflect the God of Israel. This God called their ancestor Abraham and freed them from Pharaoh. Every detail was holy, just as the Ten Commandments were holy (Brueggemann, 884). Each piece of artwork, from precise incense combinations to gold carvings, was of God's own design, imbued with divine meaning and purpose.

The artisans, however, were ordinary Israelites. They were newly freed slaves overwhelmed by the uncertainty of the wilderness. After years of captivity, only God could inspire—fill with the Spirit—the Hebrews to such imaginative artistic heights (Brueggemann, 921). Only God could give them a dream this big after years of oppression and suffering.

And only God could inspire the artisans needed to construct this work of art. In 31:2 we read that the head artisan is Bezalel, whose name means "in the shade (protection) of God." Verse 6 names his assistant as Oholiab, "my tent is the Father" (Greenstein, 136). That their names are preserved in Scripture highlights their importance and the value placed upon their gifts. The artisans' names underscore their faith in God as Israel's shelter and protector. This faith makes them fit for the job of building the place where God's presence will dwell.

Their skill sets match the task, too. God has blessed Bezalel with "divine spirit, with ability, intelligence, and knowledge in every kind of craft" (v. 4). Notice that these are not simply skills he has honed himself. Rather, God has bestowed these gifts upon him. God has given these two people the talents and the training, probably received from their Egyptian masters, to lead this project.

Further, God has given "skills to all the skillful so they may make all that I have commanded you" (v. 6). Under Bezalel and Oholiab's guidance, the Israelites will build the tabernacle with gifts God has given them. These gifts are practical wisdom (Brueggemann, 921) and artistic skill. They know how to work with various materials from stone to fabric to metal. God expects them to use their wisdom to make something that will bless God, the community, and ultimately the world as God's story spreads.

God's dwelling place on earth is designed and inspired by God but made with human hands. It is made with the stuff of earth—metals, wood, and stone—by everyday gifted people to reflect the glory of God. God creates and commands the people to join in the creation. Metalworkers, perfumers (for the oil and incense), seamstresses, weavers, woodcarvers, stonemasons, and other artisans will be part of building God's dwelling among the Israelites.

Even non-artisans participate. They offer their treasure to build the tabernacle. They also participate by feeding and caring for the artisans as they construct God's dwelling place. Later, artisans and non-artisans alike will join together in worship in the tabernacle.

God freed Israel and inspired them to build such a sanctuary. Every aspect of the tabernacle and every gift and skill of the artisans reflects God's glory. Hand-picked by God, Bezalel and Oholiab are chosen as much for their perspective as for the gifts God has given them. These skilled artisans trust the One who gave them their gifts and skills and use them for God's glory.

Understanding

God gave Moses a vision of a particular design for the tabernacle. Every detail was carefully mapped out. God told Moses exactly who to put in charge of the construction and of the skilled craftspeople "so that they may make all that I have commanded you" (31:6). God's attention to detail reflects the value of each part of the design and the value of the place itself. This was not an ordinary building. It would not look like anything the Israelites had ever seen. It would require the gifts and skills God had given to all the Israelites. It would require all of them working together to glorify God.

God received glory not just with the finished product, however. God also received glory when Moses received God's instructions and faithfully shared them with the people. It happened during the process as the Israelites used their artistic gifts to create the details that would enhance and encourage the worship of God. Together with God, at God's inspiration and direction, these newly freed slaves created a dwelling place on earth for the Almighty.

God clearly had confidence in the abilities of the Israelites. Otherwise, God would not have given them such a complicated and daunting task. During their time in Egypt, they had honed these crafts, learning the artistic trades from their oppressors. Now God called former brick-makers to become designers and creators. They stepped forward to honor the God who had given them these gifts and helped them learn these skills. Most of all, their work was informed by the God who freed them from oppression and put hope in their hearts again.

God has blessed many of us with artistic gifts. And God has blessed all of us with the ability to appreciate the work of talented artisans. Our artistic abilities, including the ability to appreciate and encourage the talents of others, are a gift from God. God gives talent and provides opportunities to develop that talent into something that blesses others and honors God in worship and in daily life.

What About Me?

• *We can honor God by using our artistic gifts.* God has blessed some of us with the same kinds of gifts for creating visual art that the Israelites used to build the tabernacle. Using these gifts to create art for worship glorifies God and may deepen worship for other believers. Seamstresses, quilters, and needleworkers can create banners, altar cloths, or costumes for dramas. Woodworkers might carve nativity scenes, crosses, or a plate and cup for the Communion table. Painters could design and paint a biblical scene for use in worship—or even paint it during worship as a visual complement to the service. During personal devotional time, all of us can be artists, drawing or doodling, coloring with crayons, or painting with oils. Our Creator God calls us to create.

• *We can honor God by appreciating the artistic gifts of others.* Even in the plainest sanctuary, visual beauty is present. In contemporary worship, we may notice how the projected image of a forest scene or beach sunrise draws our attention to God. In a more traditional sanctuary, we might pay attention to the flowers on the Communion table or the stained glass in the windows. A set of banners I recently saw depicted a dove with colors swirling around it. Their presence in a modern brick sanctuary softened the space and drew my attention to the movement of the Spirit in our worship. Where are visual arts evident in your regular worship experience?

• *Visual beauty in different artistic forms is a gift from God.* We encounter art in all kinds of places, from statues in our city or town to the student art display at the mall to the paintings and photographs for sale at an outdoor market. We see artistic beauty in jewelry handcrafted by third-world artisans, in pottery shaped by a fourth generation of potters, in baskets woven before our eyes. Each gift comes from God; each talent is shaped and each skill honed by opportunities God has afforded. The art reflects the wonder of the God who gave the gifts in the first place. Whether the artisan realizes that or not, we may recognize it and thank God for such a gift.

Resources

Walter Brueggemann, "Exodus," The New Interpreter's Bible, vol. 1 (Nashville: Abingdon, 1994).

Edward L. Greenstein, "Exodus: Introduction and Notes," *HarperCollins Study Bible* (New York: HarperCollins, 1993).

_____, "Tabernacle," *Dictionary of Bible and Religion*, ed. William H. Gentz (Nashville: Abingdon, 1986).

_____, "Tabernacle," *Mercer Dictionary of the Bible*, ed. Watson E. Mills et al. (Macon GA: Mercer University Press, 1990).

VISUAL ARTS

Exodus 31:1-11

Introduction

The novelist Vladimir Nabokov describes a spiritual awakening in one of his characters. This man is watching an old street woman drinking a cup of coffee on a cold day. As he watches her, he has one of those unexpected and blessed "aha!" moments:

> I became aware of the world's tenderness, the profound benefi-cence of all that surrounded me, the blissful bond between me and all of creation; and I realized that joy...breathed around me everywhere, in the speeding street sounds, in the hem of a comi-cally lifted skirt, in the metallic yet tender drone of the wind, in the autumn clouds bloated with rain. I realized that the world does not represent a struggle at all, or a predaceous sequence of chance events, but shimmering bliss, beneficent trepidation, a gift bestowed upon us and unappreciated. (From "Beneficence," quoted in *Books and Culture* [November/December 1995]: 26)

Any time something like that happens, we're standing on holy ground, suddenly awakened to the wonder of life. For many of us, those moments of awakening come in the presence of art. In fact, that might be a good definition for the word "art." Art is whatever awakens our spirits, helps us see "shimmering bliss," and enables us to appreciate the precious gift of life.

In this unit of study we will examine four kinds of art—visual art, musical art, literary art, and dramatic art—that gave people in the Old Testament those blessed moments of awakening.

This week we look at how God used two little-known biblical characters, Bezalel and Oholiab, to fashion "visual arts" for the tabernacle. Their artistry enabled the Israelites to sense God's presence as they came to the tabernacle to worship.

Filled with the Divine Spirit

Here's a trivia question for you: Who is the first person in the Bible described as being filled with God's spirit? We would expect the answer to that question to be Abraham, Moses, Jacob, or one of the other superstars of the Old Testament.

But the first person said to be filled with God's spirit is a little-known character named Bezalel, who wasn't a prophet or priest, but an artist. Bezalel was filled with the spirit of God "to make artistic designs for work in gold, silver, and bronze, to cut and set stones, to work in wood, and to engage in all kinds of craftsmanship" (Exod 31:5). Bezalel and his assistant, Oholiab, were to fashion works of art to make the tabernacle a place of beauty.

Bezalel and Oholiab led in the construction of the tabernacle and built the furniture that went inside it. They also designed the priestly garments the priests wore in the tabernacle and extended their influence by teaching their art to others. Evidently, they were multi-gifted artists, able to fashion their art in a variety of media—gold, silver, bronze, stone, and wood.

It was—and probably still is—a shocking thought that a workman, an artist, would receive the spirit of God to do his work. In the cultures of Greece and Rome, manual labor was despised. It was thought to be work for slaves, not free citizens. But in Hebrew thought, manual labor was honored and esteemed. So, here in Exodus, we read about Bezalel and Oholiab doing the work of God by working with their hands, fashioning things of beauty to go in the tabernacle.

We need to know about these men because they remind us that God fills people with his spirit to do more than "religious things." We often think of God as calling people to be preachers, missionaries, youth ministers, or Bible teachers. Certainly, God can and does call people to serve in those capacities.

But, as we will see throughout this unit of study, God calls people to be artists, musicians, writers, and dramatists too. The spirit of God blows where it will, and it sometimes inspires people like Bezalel and Oholiab to create their art so that the rest of us can have moments of worship and awakening.

When we gaze at the work of modern-day Bezalels and Oholiabs, two positive things can happen to us. First, we can feel the "fire" of the artist and find our inner fire rekindled, and, second, we can be challenged to use our particular gifts to the glory of God.

Feeling the Fire

Vincent van Gogh, the great Dutch painter, once wrote,

> There may be a great fire in your soul, yet no one ever comes to warm himself at it, and the passersby only see a wisp of smoke coming through the chimney, and go along their way. Look here, now what must be done? Must one tend the inner fire, have salt in one-self, wait patiently yet with how much impatience for the hour when somebody will come and sit down—maybe to stay? Let him who believes in God wait for the hour that will come sooner or later. (Quoted in Henri Nouwen, *The Way of the Heart* [New York: Ballantine, 1981] 39)

We can only imagine the situation that prompted that statement. No doubt van Gogh often felt that people passed by his work without stopping to appreciate it. He felt that they never warmed themselves by the fire of his work. When you've expressed your "insides" on canvas, paper, or stage and no one pays attention, it is not a fun experience. Every artist probably knows that frustration.

What is an artist, writer, composer, or actor to do in such a situation? Van Gogh's answer is "tend the inner fire, have salt in one-self, wait patiently...for the hour when someone will come and stay." The artist's task is to keep the inner fire alive so that those with "ears to hear" and "eyes to see" can have their own fires rekindled.

Robert Frost once said that poetry begins with a lump in the throat. But so do painting, writing, singing, acting, and all other arts. The artist has an experience that puts a lump in his or her throat, and then runs to the canvas, computer, or concert hall to express that experience.

American novelist Willa Cather once told a young painter named Grant Reynard, "The crux of this whole art experience is in the word *desire*—an urgent need to *recreate* a vital life experience which wells up within and must find expression in the writing" (quoted in Bruce Lockerbie, *The Timeless Moment* [Westchester IL: Cornerstone, 1980] 16). If the artist is truly an artist, those of us who see and hear and experience the art get lumps in our throats, too.

In her book *Walking on Water*, Madeleine L'Engle wrote, "When we are writing, or painting, or composing, we are, during the time of creativity, freed from normal restrictions, and are opened to a wider world, where colors are brighter, sounds clearer, and people more wonderfully complex than we normally realize" (New York: Bantam, 1980, p. 101). When we read a poem, see a painting, listen to a composition, or watch a play, we, too, are opened to a wider world, and at least for that moment we get to see and hear things we don't ordinarily see and hear. In the presence of art, the fire within us gets rekindled.

My Own Particular Gift

I recently attended an art show for a good friend who is a fine painter of portraits and landscapes. As I wandered around the gallery, admiring Bill's paintings, two thoughts hit me almost simultaneously.

First, I thought about how gifted he is as an artist. Even though he is a good friend and I am certainly biased, I think Bill is a fine painter. Walking through the gallery that evening confirmed that fact for me.

Second, I thought about how *not* gifted I am as an artist. Put a canvas before me, and the best I can produce are stick figures that look like something a first-grader would draw. When God distributed artistic ability, I must have been out of the room. My mother was a painter, and our house is filled with her work. Evidently, she didn't pass any of those art genes along to her son.

But being in the presence of my friend's artistic ability didn't depress me; it reminded me that I have gifts, too, and that I am called to use the gifts I *do* have. I *can* write a decent sentence and have written some books I hope have both substance and style. I can strum the guitar and sing on key. And I *can* craft a sermon that mostly makes sense. You might laugh at my attempts to produce visual art, but I hope you would find my musical and literary artwork compelling. I don't have many gifts, but I am supposed to use the ones I have to the glory of God.

"To try to talk about art and about Christianity," L'Engle wrote, "is for me one and the same thing, and it means attempting to share the meaning of my life, what gives it, for me, its tragedy and its glory. It is what makes me respond to the death of an apple tree, the birth of a puppy, northern lights shaking the sky..." (*Walking on Water*, 16).

Some, like my friend Bill, attempt to share the meaning of their lives by daubing paint on canvas. Some play the piano, write poems, act in plays, cook casseroles, or run marathons. Whatever our gifts, we take them, dedicate ourselves to them, and offer them to God.

Walking by my friend's fine paintings at the art show didn't intimidate me at all. His paintings inspired me to take my own gifts and quietly put them on display, too.

Conclusion

Henri Nouwen once saw a reproduction of Rembrandt's painting *The Return of the Prodigal Son* and became fascinated by the work. A few years later he traveled to Russia to see the original painting in The Hermitage in Saint Petersburg.

As you would imagine, the original was even more breathtaking than the poster reproduction. Nouwen said he was so transfixed by the painting that he pulled up a chair and gazed at it for four hours. For him, looking at that painting was a life-changing experience.

He later wrote a book about the experience, and he titled it simply *The Return of the Prodigal Son*. He concludes that book by saying,

> When four years ago, I went to Saint Petersburg to see Rembrandt's *The Return of the Prodigal Son*, I had little idea how much I would have to live what I then saw. I stand with awe at the place where Rembrandt brought me. He led me from the kneeling, disheveled young son to the standing, bent-over old father, from the place of being blessed to the place of blessing. As I look at my own aging hands, I know that they have been

given to me to stretch out toward all who suffer, to rest upon the shoulders of all who come, and to offer the blessing that emerges from the immensity of God's love. (New York: Doubleday, 1994, p. 139)

Perhaps we should take this lesson about Bezalel and Oholiab, hurry over to the nearest art museum, and see if something similar can happen to us. Perhaps in the presence of genuine art, we will feel again the fire in our own soul, and maybe we will even be encouraged to produce our own art.

It is entirely possible that something like that happened to the people of Israel as they went to the tabernacle to worship and saw what Bezalel and Oholiab had made. They saw their spirit-led works of art and, in the process, caught a fresh glimpse of the God who inspired it.

Notes

Notes

2

MUSICAL ARTS

1 Samuel 16:14-23

Central Question

What is the role of music in my relationship with God?

Scripture

1 Samuel 16:14-23 14 Now the spirit of the LORD departed from Saul, and an evil spirit from the LORD tormented him. 15 And Saul's servants said to him, "See now, an evil spirit from God is tormenting you. 16 Let our lord now command the servants who attend you to look for someone who is skillful in playing the lyre; and when the evil spirit from God is upon you, he will play it, and you will feel better." 17 So Saul said to his servants, "Provide for me someone who can play well, and bring him to me." 18 One of the young men answered, "I have seen a son of Jesse the Bethlehemite who is skillful in playing, a man of valor, a warrior, prudent in speech, and a man of good presence; and the Lord is with him." 19 So Saul sent messengers to Jesse, and said, "Send me your son David who is with the sheep." 20 Jesse took a donkey loaded with bread, a skin of wine, and a kid, and sent them by his son David to Saul. 21 And David came to Saul, and entered his service. Saul loved him greatly, and he became his armor-bearer. 22 Saul sent to Jesse, saying, "Let David remain in my service, for he has found favor in my sight." 23 And whenever the evil spirit from God came upon Saul, David took the lyre and played it with his hand, and Saul would be relieved and feel better, and the evil spirit would depart from him.

Reflecting

"When words fail, music speaks," reads a bumper sticker proudly displayed on the car of an old friend. Many of us can identify with that sentiment. Whether we are musicians or music lovers, many believers sense that music is an international language that powerfully connects us to each other and to God.

As a former chaplain in a skilled nursing facility, I witnessed the power of music over and over. Residents who rarely spoke or were lost in their own mental worlds would often respond when they heard music. Sometimes it would be a popular favorite from their past. Strains of "In the Mood" began, and soon smiles appeared and heads bobbed in time to the music. The music of old favorites also brought back memories of earlier days.

Other times we would sing a familiar hymn—"The Old Rugged Cross" or "Amazing Grace"—and voices that rarely made a sound would join in. Those old hymns touched a place deep within, resurrecting melody and even words in those who had known them by heart. When the music ended, the atmosphere of the activity room had changed. We were no longer a gathering of individuals but one body connected through music and spirit. In a place many people dismiss as sad and lonely, our hearts were gladdened and joined by the miracle of music.

> **?** Are there songs that always make you glad? Are there songs that always make you feel sentimental?

Today's text shows that God indeed works through music on many different levels. Young David's gifts as a musician soothe King Saul as he struggles with mental and emotional torment. Though the two later become estranged, here we see the current and future kings connected by the gift of music.

Studying

Little did David know that his reputation as a lyre-player and singer would bring him into the king's court, the center of Israel's political power. But when the court servants see King Saul struggling, their first instinct is to soothe him with music. One of the servants thinks of David and gives him a recommendation that goes far beyond his skills as a musician. The young shepherd is quickly called to attend the king of Israel.

Saul was not always in torment. Earlier in 1 Samuel, we read that after Saul's anointing, Samuel promises "the spirit of the LORD will possess you" (10:5-6). This language conveys God's special favor and blessing. But God is clear that if Saul or Israel should turn from God's ways, God will "be against you and your king" (12:14-15). Having the spirit of the Lord depends on obedience and faithfulness.

Saul makes two decisions that break God's commands. First, he makes a sacrifice before battle that should have been offered by Samuel. He thus takes on the rights and responsibilities of a priest and prophet (1 Sam 13:5-15). Samuel speaks against Saul: "now your kingdom will not continue; the LORD has sought out a man after his own heart" (13:14).

Later, Saul rebels against God's command a second time. After defeating the Amalekites, Saul breaks God's command to completely destroy the enemy and all their belongings (15:1-3). Though this seems like a harsh practice in our modern perspective, God's command reflected that everything won in battle was to be an offering to the Lord (McCarter, 440). Saul spares the Amalekite king, however, and keeps the best of the enemies' herds and valuables. Samuel is appalled. "Because you have rejected the LORD," he says, "the LORD has rejected you as king" (15:23).

God directs Samuel to anoint secretly a new king, one of Jesse's sons (16:1). The chosen king is the youngest, David, in whom God saw the right heart for kingship (16:7). When the young man was anointed, "the spirit of the LORD came mightily upon David from that day forward" (16:13)—though he would not assume the throne for some time.

Apparently, there can only be one spirit-anointed leader at a given time. Once David is anointed, the spirit of the Lord departs from Saul. Not only that, but an "evil spirit from the LORD tormented him" (16:14). The attribution of the evil spirit to God underscores that Saul's affliction has a "spiritual aspect," mirroring his alienation from God and God's spirit because of his own choices (Birch, 1102; Brueggemann, 125). His continued disobedience as king has separated him from God. This breach results in political, spiritual, and physical turmoil.

Saul's servants recognize the torment of their king and immediately prescribe music as the cure (vv. 15-16). This response points toward an ancient awareness of the connection between music and a person's spiritual life. Saul quickly accepts their prescription, requesting that they bring him someone who "can play well" (v. 17).

A young servant is ready with an answer, suggesting a "son of Jesse the Bethlehemite who is skillful in playing" (v. 18). He goes on to list David's other attributes, which have little to do with music. But the most important is that "the LORD is with him" (v. 18). No one notices the irony that, while "an evil spirit from the LORD" torments Saul, they are inviting a young man favored by God's spirit into Saul's court. Perhaps they are simply that desperate for a cure.

Saul sends messengers to Jesse asking for David, describing him as the one "who is with the sheep" (v. 19). Apparently, Saul knows quite a bit about David. Jesse responds by sending David along with gifts for the king (v. 20). Saul grows to love David and asks Jesse if David can remain in the king's service (vv. 21-22).

David's music calms Saul. He would play, and "Saul would be relieved and feel better, and the evil spirit would depart from him" (v. 23). The secretly anointed king brings comfort to the present king. It is a sign of things to come. This musician later uses his skills to bless all of Israel—and later all the church— through the Psalms.

Understanding

As his close companions, Saul's court attendants were aware of his turmoil and wanted to help. They turned to music. There were probably many musicians who could play for Saul. But as God would have it, someone had heard of David's skills as a musician and his character as a young man with many admirable qualities.

Saul apparently agreed that music might help him, given how quickly he took up the servants' idea. Interestingly, years earlier, just after his own anointing as king, Saul joined a group of musicians in a "prophetic frenzy" and "the spirit of God possessed him" (10:5-13). Saul knew the power of music in his own spiritual life, especially as a source of inspiration.

At least temporarily, David's music brought solace and healing. His playing relieved Saul and helped him feel better. It also made the evil spirit depart (16:23). That is powerful music! In this story, music soothes, relieves, *and* drives away evil spirits. Clearly, God still cared for Saul. God sent David to bless him with the gift of music.

Many of us know the healing power of music in big and small ways. Some of us play music in the car to set the tone for wherever we are going: upbeat music to begin the day, calming music to unwind on the way home. The surprise of hearing a favorite song on the radio has encouraged many a listener for the day ahead.

In the deep valleys of life, music can play a vital role. For example, at funerals, music reminds us of God's promises and evokes memories of the loved one we have lost. Singing "Standing on the Promises" reminds me of standing next to my grandfather in a little country church, listening to him belt out those assuring words.

You may have songs and hymns that remind you of certain people or certain times in your life. These are a gift from God.

What About Me?

• *Music can be the God-shaped soundtrack of our lives.* Remember the songs you sang as a kid? At a recent ministers' meeting, several adults chimed in during the chorus of a musical they had all learned as kids at different churches. We laughed at how many of the words they remembered! The songs that spoke to us as children still speak to us today, eliciting memories and feelings. The same is true for the music from our teenage years, the song from our wedding, or the tunes we sang to our babies. God has used these songs to compose our lives.

• *God can use music to bridge generations and cultures.* I was buying vacuum bags at Sears when a decades-old song came on the radio behind the counter. I laughed, commenting, "I haven't heard this song in forever!" The multi-pierced, gum-smacking clerk said, "Yeah, it's a golden oldie," and we both sang along softly while my credit card went through. That put a smile on my face and hers, too. In a much more powerful way, music can join cultures as some of us learn to love salsa music and others the sound of African drums. The music of Christians all over the world reflects particular cultures, inviting us to remember the lesson from the children's chorus: "Every color, every race, all are covered by His grace."

• *Let music speak in your life.* Saint Augustine is reported to have said the one who sings prays twice. Music can be a vital part of our relationship with God. Some of us find personal devotional time enriched by prayerfully listening to or singing a favorite spiritual song—modern, ancient, or straight from the hymnal. "Good" singing voices are not required. All we need is willingness to use music to draw closer to God. If you sing in the shower, you can sing to God! If you are a musician, allow your playing or singing to be an offering for God, whether in corporate worship or practice. However we choose to invite music more deeply into our lives, we will find ourselves blessed, since (in the words of Martin Luther) "music is a fair and glorious gift of God."

Resources

Bruce C. Birch, "I and II Samuel," *The New Interpreter's Bible*, vol. 2 (Nashville: Abingdon, 1998).

Walter Brueggemann, "I and II Samuel," *Interpretation* (Louisville KY: John Knox, 1990).

James M. Efird, *The Old Testament Writings: History, Literature, Interpretation* (Atlanta: John Knox, 1982).

P. Kyle McCarter Jr., "I Samuel: Introduction and Notes," *HarperCollins Study Bible* (New York: HarperCollins, 1993).

Ben F. Philbeck Jr., "I and II Samuel," *Broadman Bible Commentary* (Nashville: Broadman, 1970).

MUSICAL ARTS

1 Samuel 16:14-23

Introduction

The Bible is filled with the sound of music. Over 1,100 verses in Scripture make reference to music. To read the Bible is to read about horns, trumpets, lyres, harps, cymbals, drums, psalms, laments, and voices lifted in song.

You might want to introduce this lesson on the musical arts by giving your class a pop quiz on music in the Bible.

• What type of instrument did David play to soothe Saul? (harp or lyre—1 Sam 16:23)
• What book of the Bible is an ancient Hebrew hymnal? (Psalms)
• What instrument does the prophet Amos say strikes fear into the hearts of the people when they hear it? (trumpet—Amos 3:6)
• Who in the Old Testament was the father of all who play the harp and flute? (Jubal—Gen 4:21)
• In the book of Revelation, about what city does the angel say, "the sound of harpists and minstrels and of flutists and trumpeters will be heard in you no more"? (Babylon—Rev 18:22)
• What instrument did Miriam play to celebrate the crossing of the Red Sea? (cymbals—Ex 15:20)
• What did Paul encourage the Colossian Christians to sing? (psalms, hymns, and spiritual songs—Col 3:16)

That's a small sampling of the music mentioned in Scripture. In this lesson, we look at an Old Testament story about Saul and David as a way to remind ourselves of some of the ways music stirs our souls and brings us closer to God.

Saul's Evil Spirit

"Now the spirit of the LORD departed from Saul, and an evil spirit from the LORD tormented him" (1 Sam 16:14). In the first verse of this passage, we are confronted with a dilemma: *God* sent the evil spirit to Saul? *God* is responsible for his torment?

At this early point in the development of Israel's faith, people did not think in terms of Satan as later generations would. To them, God was responsible for everything that happened. Thus, God could be described as hardening Pharaoh's heart (Exod 7:3), sending a lying spirit to a prophet (1 Kgs 22:22), or even attempting to kill Moses (Exod 4:24). In the minds of the early biblical writers, God intervened in human history for specific reasons. In their minds, God's hand was everywhere.

The historian who wrote 1 Samuel saw God's hand in the entire story of David and Saul. God brought about Saul's torment and depression so that David could be introduced into the life of Israel and eventually become its king. It started with an evil spirit from the Lord and ended with the accession of David as ruler of the land.

Saul's servants suggested that he find someone to play the lyre (a stringed instrument similar to a harp) to make him feel better. One young servant even had a suggestion: "I have seen a son of Jesse the Bethlehemite who is skillful in playing, a man of valor, a warrior, prudent in speech, and a man of good presence; and the Lord is with him" (1 Sam 16:18).

Saul dispatched a messenger to Jesse asking that his son David, the shepherd-boy, be sent to him. Jesse loaded a donkey with provisions and sent David on his way. David went to Saul and became an immediate favorite. The writer says, "Saul loved him greatly" (1 Sam 16:21). David became Saul's full-time assistant and armor bearer—preparing the way for the story of David and Goliath in chapter 17.

David's musical skills were definitely helpful to a tormented Saul. The biblical writer explains, "And whenever the evil spirit came upon Saul, David took the lyre and played it with his hand, and Saul would be relieved and feel better, and the evil spirit would depart from him" (1 Sam 16:23).

Under the influence of gentle harp music, Saul's spirit was calmed, and he could better cope with his demons. The picture of Saul being comforted by David's playing reminds us of one of the great benefits of good music: it soothes our spirits and enables us to cope in a loud, crazy world.

The Soothing Sound of Music

Our family had its own version of this story several years ago. My mother had Alzheimer's and occasionally had times when she was agitated and disturbed. Like Saul, Mom had her own "evil spirit," and, like him, she was in torment when that spirit came upon her.

But my father learned how to put her at ease. When she became unusually disturbed, Dad would get a portable tape recorder from the bedroom closet and play a tape of Mom's favorite hymns. The effect was immediate and almost hypnotic. Under the spell of "What a Friend We Have in Jesus" and "Whispering Hope," Mom grew visibly more relaxed and peaceful. Those familiar songs did for her what David's lyre did for Saul. They eased her torment, "and the evil spirit would depart from [her]."

What one of us hasn't had a similar experience? We might not have Alzheimer's or feel afflicted with an evil spirit, but we do know what it's like to feel tormented by pressure, conflict, and grief. In those moments of trouble, one of our best allies is the soothing sound of good music.

After a long day at the office, listening to Bach or Beethoven might be what the doctor ordered. After dealing with rambunctious kids all day, the sounds of soft jazz might be heavenly. And after returning from the funeral home, the best medicine for our grief might be a recording of a great choir singing the classic hymns of the church.

Many of those great hymns were written precisely for the purpose of soothing our souls, ridding us of our evil spirits, and quieting us so we can hear God. Open any hymnal, and you will find those songs—"Amazing Grace," "It Is Well with My Soul," "Abide with Me," "When I Survey the Wondrous Cross," and dozens of others.

One of the true benefits of music, whether played on a harp or an electronic device, is that it can escort us into a quieter world. In that quieter world, we can experience what is Holy.

The Clarion Call of Music

More years ago than I like to admit, I ran my one and only marathon. It was the Woodlands Marathon near Houston, and I ran it in just under four hours. I must say, though, it was not an enjoyable experience. If someone ever tells you a person "hits the wall" at about mile twenty of a marathon, believe him. At about mile twenty, I lost all interest in the race. It was as if my brain said to my body, "I've had it. You can keep going if you want to, but I'm checking out."

Fortunately, I was running with a friend. He suggested we walk for a while and then see how we felt. I walked a bit and started feeling better. We even began to jog slowly toward the finish line and got close enough to hear a wonderful sound: the theme song from the movie *Rocky* blaring from a loud speaker. I knew then the finish line was close, and with the strains of *Rocky* giving rhythm to my tired feet, I crossed the line with a flourish. My friend and the music got me to the finish line.

That underscores the second way music brings us closer to God. It inspires us, challenges us, and energizes us. If music has the power to soothe our frazzled spirits, it also has the power to fortify our spirits when they are fatigued. That's why the bugler plays just before the cavalry charges. That's why the band plays as the football team is driving for the go-ahead score. That's why the organist pulls out all the stops on "Messiah." Music has the incredible power to "fire us up."

In an obscure passage in the book of 2 Kings, the prophet Elisha is asked by the kings of Israel, Judah, and Edom to give them a prophecy. Elisha seems disinterested and befuddled by their request but asks them to give him a musician. Second Kings 3:15 says, "And then, while the musician was playing, the power of the LORD came on him." Elisha, having received clarity and energy through the music, then gives the kings the prophecy they need.

Hymnal compilers know about music's power to energize and inspire, and every hymnal includes songs of that sort: "Onward Christian Soldiers," "Victory in Jesus," "Here I Am, Lord," and many more. Thanks to some of those songs, we often leave church revitalized and ready to take on the world for Christ.

The Teaching Role of Music

For years I've carried my guitar to the Alzheimer's center across the street from our church and led a monthly worship service for the residents there. Inevitably, I play the old songs like "The Old Rugged Cross," "This Little Light of Mine," "Do Lord," and "He's Got the Whole World in His Hands." Most of the people in the center have severe memory problems, but the very people who can't remember what they had for lunch that day can sing these old songs without ever looking at the song sheet. It's as if the songs got permanently embedded in their memory and will be the last thing to leave.

Music has staying power and, for that reason, it is one of our best teaching tools. Give a child a sermon, and he or she will forget it in an hour. Give a child a song, and he or she might be singing it seventy years later in a retirement center. The third way music brings us closer to God is that it carries indelible truth in its tunes and lyrics.

No one knew that better than the Old Testament Jews who taught their children early on to sing the psalms. Those psalms were more than ditties to pass the time of day on a long trip. They were musical Sunday school lessons, teaching both children and adults what a life of faith looks like. Anyone enrolled in the psalm choir would be a better-than-average theologian.

Though it pains me to admit it, I know that the songs we sing in our church every Sunday teach people more, and stick with people longer, than the sermons I preach. Music has always been one of humanity's greatest teachers.

Conclusion

Most people don't know that the renowned composer Johann Sebastian Bach was a church musician. Bach was the choirmaster and musical director of Saint Thomas's Church and School in Leipzig, Germany, in the early 1700s. Nearly three-fourths of his 1,000 compositions were written for use in worship.

His ministry at the church was filled with conflict and disillusionment. Most in the church didn't appreciate Bach's musical genius and thought of him as a stuffy old man who stubbornly clung to obsolete forms of music. But Bach kept writing and leading the music, sometimes writing a cantata a week, 202 of which survive.

Some eighty years after his death, Bach was "discovered" when the composer Felix Mendelssohn arranged a performance of Bach's *The Passion of St. Matthew*. For most of his life, though, Bach was a church music director, toiling away in relative obscurity and dealing with dissension.

At the age of forty-eight, Bach received a copy of Luther's three-volume translation of the Bible. He pored over it as if it were a long-lost treasure map. When he came to 2 Chronicles 5:13, which speaks of the temple musicians praising God, he noted in the margin, "At a reverent performance of music, God is always at hand with his gracious presence" (quoted in *131 Christians Everyone Should Know* [Nashville: Broadman & Holman, 2000] 109).

Bach succinctly summed up the magic of music. God uses music to soothe us, energize us, and teach us. Through the gift of good music, "God is always at hand with his gracious presence," filling our lives with comfort, strength, and truth.

Notes

Notes

3

LITERARY ARTS

2 Samuel 12:1-9

Central Question

How does the written word help me learn more about God?

Scripture

2 Samuel 12:1-9 1 and the LORD sent Nathan to David. He came to him, and said to him, "There were two men in a certain city, the one rich and the other poor. 2 The rich man had very many flocks and herds; 3 but the poor man had nothing but one little ewe lamb, which he had bought. He brought it up, and it grew up with him and with his children; it used to eat of his meager fare, and drink from his cup, and lie in his bosom, and it was like a daughter to him. 4 Now there came a traveler to the rich man, and he was loath to take one of his own flock or herd to prepare for the wayfarer who had come to him, but he took the poor man's lamb, and prepared that for the guest who had come to him." 5 Then David's anger was greatly kindled against the man. He said to Nathan, "As the LORD lives, the man who has done this deserves to die; 6 he shall restore the lamb fourfold, because he did this thing, and because he had no pity." 7 Nathan said to David, "You are the man! Thus says the LORD, the God of Israel: I anointed you king over Israel, and I rescued you from the hand of Saul; 8 I gave you your master's house, and your master's wives into your bosom, and gave you the house of Israel and of Judah; and if that had been too little, I would have added as much more. 9 Why have you despised the word of the LORD, to do what is evil in his sight? You have struck down Uriah the Hittite with the sword, and have taken his wife to be your wife, and have killed him with the sword of the Ammonites."

Reflecting

"Tell me a story." It's a request heard around the world wherever children are preparing for bed. Its close cousin, "Read me a story," drives the billion-dollar publishing industry. Books, articles, and stories are downloaded from the Internet every second: evidence that adults like hearing a story as much as children do.

Storytelling is an ancient art. It's humanity's millennia-old way of conveying events, making a point, and educating one another. Until the advent of the written word, the spoken word said it all, at campfires and courts and places of worship. The nature of this oral culture required people to specialize in memorizing stories in order to teach morality and laws, history and culture. The development of writing allowed these stories to be recorded. They were then more readily shared between cultures and generations.

One gift of a story is that we can hear ourselves in its characters. For a while, we get to see through their perspective or the narrator's. Often the events of the story ring true in our lives. We imagine ourselves reacting to what the characters face.

That's what happened when King David heard Nathan's story. God sent Nathan the prophet to confront David about his sin against Bathsheba and her husband, Uriah the Hittite—a highly unenviable task. But Nathan wisely approached David not with prophetic zeal but with a story. The story helped David see his sin in the actions of a make-believe character. The story changed David's life, just as Jesus' parables would later change the lives of millions.

> **?** What non-biblical stories have helped shape your character and outlook on life? *The Velveteen Rabbit? Hamlet? Harry Potter?* What makes these stories so influential?

Studying

King David has long enjoyed the favor of the Lord, beginning with his secret anointing as Israel's king (1 Sam 16:13). Yet God has always been clear that David, along with all of Israel, is called to keep covenant with God (1 Sam 12:14-15). Breaking the covenant and turning from God's ways is not acceptable behavior for any

Israelite—including the king. At the same time, God is also clear that David's sins will not remove God's love from him. It will, however, result in discipline as a father disciplines a beloved child (2 Sam 7:14-15).

David puts God's promise to the test when he takes Uriah the Hittite's wife, Bathsheba, sleeps with her, and sends her home. When he finds out she is pregnant, he contrives to get Uriah, his loyal soldier, to go home to lie with his wife so everyone will assume the child is Uriah's. But Uriah will not cooperate. He has taken to heart the commandments against enjoying the comforts of home while Israel is at battle. So to cover up his first sin, David commits another: murder. He sends a secret message by Uriah's own hand to General Joab, ordering him to abandon Uriah in the fighting and thus ensure his death (2 Sam 11).

Coveting, lying, adultery, murder, abuse of power...the list goes on. David's power as king has numbed him to the power of his own sin—and to the reality that all Israelites are subject to God's law. Once Bathsheba has completed her period of mourning for Uriah, David marries her, thinking he is done with the matter.

But God is *not* done with the matter, as the final verse of chapter 11 attests: "But the thing that David had done displeased the LORD" (11:27). God sends Nathan the prophet to confront David about his sin. Nathan was introduced earlier when he offered an oracle about David's dynasty lasting forever (7:16). Now he makes his second appearance. This time he comes to pronounce a judgment against that same king.

Confronting the most powerful man in the land, the king chosen by God, was a tough task. In having Uriah killed, David has already proven that he will use his power to get rid of those who don't conform to his wishes. Now God tells Nathan to confront him. Nathan proceeds at great personal risk.

The prophet uses the ancient art of storytelling in his confrontation. Instead of starting with an oracle of judgment, he chooses an innocuous story about something that might have happened. A rich man steals a poor man's pet lamb to feed an unexpected guest. The rich man has plenty, but he ruthlessly takes the thing dearest to the poor man. What he does is heartless, but it is also illegal according to the hospitality laws of the day. A person might take from a neighbor's herd if he had no herd of his own, but he could *not* take a neighbor's pet (McCarter, 483)!

Immediately David identifies the sin in the story. He says the rich man's action is wrong and names the sinful attitude behind it: "he had no pity" (v. 6). David passes quick judgment on the

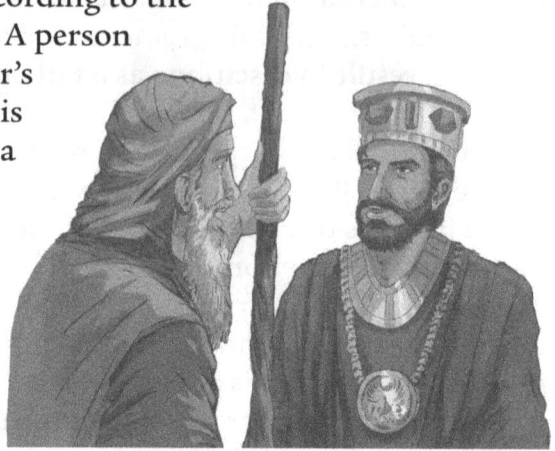
Nathan and David

rich man, saying he should restore the lamb fourfold, in keeping with Exodus 22:1. But notice that he starts with "the man who has done this deserves to die" (v. 5). David feels strongly about the injustice done to the poor man.

Now that David's sense of justice is in play, Nathan states his accusation: "You are the man!" These four words (two words in Hebrew) rip open the closed book of David's sin. Having already judged the character in the story, David cannot excuse his own similar behavior. Now that David is in the right frame of heart and mind, the oracle of judgment begins. God reminds David that God has been the one to anoint him, rescue him, and give him homes and wives and the house of Israel and Judah (vv. 7-8). In response to these blessings, David did "what is evil in the sight of the LORD" (v. 9).

> When someone steals an ox or a sheep, and slaughters it or sells it, the thief shall pay five oxen for an ox, and four sheep for a sheep. (Exodus 22:1)

Nathan allowed David the chance to hear the truth of his own story in the words of another story. Just as Jesus used parables centuries later, Nathan used a story to speak truth at an angle, taking a kinder approach than a direct accusation. Once David could hear the painful truth in the story, he could hear God's truth in his life. Only then could he confess, repent, and be forgiven.

Understanding

Hearing the cold, hard truth is never easy. Our human tendency is to cover our sins and protect our perceived weak spots. Often we go out of our way to avoid looking at ourselves directly. We certainly don't appreciate anyone else pointing out what we've worked hard to ignore or hide. Yet we spend far more energy covering the truth than we do when we actually face it.

That was Nathan's gift to David: he told him the truth when no one else would. Nathan's other gift was telling David the truth in a less threatening way—through a story. It is usually easier to hear the wrongs in a character's actions than in our own. The words "once upon a time" or "there once was a man" invite us into a story removed from ours. From that comfortable distance, we can see more clearly, engage our imaginations, and expand our minds. The story isn't directly about us.

At the same time, the story connects with us enough to speak to us. Nathan's story connected to David's life enough that David eventually could not deny the parallels. The tale of the rich man and poor man opened the necessary space in David's life for him to consider what pain such a pitiless action would create. He never saw or admitted the pain his own actions created until he heard the story.

In God's hands, a story—whether spoken or written—has the power to pull away our blinders and allow us to think from a different perspective. Only then do we often notice truths

In 2006 *The New York Times* polled prominent writers, critics, editors, and others in the literary world for their vote for the best work of American fiction in the last twenty-five years. The results:

Winner
Toni Morrison, *Beloved* (1987)

Runners-up
Don DeLillo, *Underworld* (1997)
Cormac McCarthy, *Blood Meridian* (1985)
John Updike, *Rabbit Angstrom: The Four Novels* (1971–1985)
Philip Roth, *American Pastoral* (1997)

we had not previously seen. God can use all sorts of stories to shape and challenge us.

What About Me?

• *Think about the stories God has used to speak to you.* From our earliest bedtime stories to last week's great read, God uses story to mold us. How has God used oral and written stories to shape you? You might revisit a favorite childhood story. That book you read for your high school term paper may say something different to you as an adult. Are there magazines you look forward to reading every time they arrive in your mailbox? Are there books you keep coming back to? Why? What do these stories offer you? How does God use them to convict, inspire, and call to you?

• *Even people who don't consider themselves readers are affected by the Word.* Remember that Jesus is the Word of God. This ancient name for Jesus comes from the Greek *logos*, the "divine principle of reason that gives order to the universe and links the human mind to the mind of God" (Rensberger, 2013). The Word may be found in all sorts of words, written and oral: the stories our grandparents told us, the stories about our own childhood, and the stories that capture our imaginations. Consider the stories that have captured your imagination—from a comic book character's story to fairy tales to memoirs from a favorite hero. How has—and how might—the Word of God speak to you through these?

• *Revive the old book report idea and give it an appealing twist.* Many of us are always looking for a new book or article to read or a compelling story to hear. Use your class time or arrange another time for people to share about the written and oral stories that have shaped their lives. No written reports or uncomfortable presentations are required! Each person simply brings a story, book, or article to show the others and offers a brief word on how God has spoken through this story. The shared pieces need not be overtly "religious," and the effects don't need to be hugely life-changing. Think of friends sharing over coffee in a casual inviting atmosphere. Think of Jesus telling a story to his friends.

Resources

Bruce C. Birch, "I and II Samuel," *The New Interpreter's Bible*, vol. 2 (Nashville: Abingdon, 1998).

P. Kyle McCarter Jr., "I and II Samuel: Introduction and Notes," *HarperCollins Study Bible* (New York: HarperCollins, 1993).

David K. Rensberger, "John: Notes," *HarperCollins Study Bible* (New York: HarperCollins, 1993).

LITERARY ARTS

2 Samuel 12:1-9

Introduction

In his book *The Timeless Moment*, Bruce Lockerbie writes, "I am coming to know this about myself: I write for the same reason I breathe—not because I choose to, but because I'm compelled to write in order to *be*. I breathe in, I breathe out; the experience of life is my inspiration, writing about it my expiration" (Westchester IL: Cornerstone, 1980, p. 81).

Thank God (literally!) there are countless people like that: gifted writers who inhale experience and exhale words. Thank God there are wordsmiths who can express what the rest of us feel but cannot convey in words. Thank God there are gifted practitioners of the literary arts—poets, preachers, novelists, essayists, and others—who inspire, challenge, entertain, and teach us.

Finding Ourselves in the Story

Our passage for this week reminds us of the power of stories, how words can get inside our minds and hearts and make us different people.

The story Nathan tells in 2 Samuel 12 is a simple one. Two men—a rich man and a poor man—lived in the same city. The rich man had many flocks and herds; the poor man had nothing but a little ewe lamb, and that lamb was like a daughter to him. The lamb ate from his table, drank from his cup, and liked to nestle in his lap.

A certain hungry traveler came to that city. The rich man decided not to take one of his many sheep but rather to take the poor man's precious lamb and use it to feed the traveler.

The cruelty and injustice of that act is obvious. David responded to Nathan's tale right on cue: "As the LORD lives, the man who has done this deserves to die; he shall restore the lamb fourfold, because he did this thing, and because he had no pity" (2 Sam 12:5-6).

Then Nathan drove his point home. "You are the man!" he said, no doubt wagging his finger at David. He went on to catalog David's obvious cruelties and injustices: greed, pride, trickery, adultery, and murder. David had done precisely what the rich man had done. He had trampled on the rights and feelings of others to get his own way.

That story became more than a story; it became a mirror in which David saw his ugly, sinful image. That story did for David what all good writing does for us: it enabled him to see himself with new eyes.

Nathan's story had three qualities that seem to characterize all effective writing. First, it was honest. Nathan spoke straight from his heart, confronting David with the truth. All good writing has that quality. When we read quality literature, we sense we're in the presence of a writer committed to telling the truth at all costs.

Second, it was simple. Nathan's story was so simple a child could understand it. But that's part of its effectiveness. When it comes to writing, the simpler the better.

Third, it was creative. Nathan's story caught David by surprise, and good literature does that. It gives us a fresh angle on truth. It gives us a fresh set of images to put in our brains. Good writing either gives us new truth to consider, or it presents old truth in a fresh way.

As we examine the literary arts in this lesson, let's use Nathan's story to probe the three qualities of good writing. We know we're in the presence of literary art when we find words that are honest, simple, and creative.

An Honest Word

E. B. White, once wrote, "Why else would you be reading this fragmentary page—you with the book on your lap? You're not out to learn anything, certainly. You just want the healing action of some chance corroboration, the soporific of spirit laid against spirit" (*One Man's Meat* [New York: Harper & Row, 1938] 79).

There are probably times when we go to a book to learn something, but most of the time I think E. B. White is right. We read hoping to meet a kindred spirit, hoping an honest writer will lay his or her spirit next to ours. We're all searching the world for honest people who will share their hearts with us. Good writers do that.

The great sportswriter Red Smith once said, "Writing is easy. All you do is sit down at a typewriter and open up a vein" (quoted by Jon Winokur, *Advice to Writers* [New York: Pantheon, 1999] 24). Good writing bleeds onto the page. When we read the words of a good writer, we sense we are in the presence of a real human being who is not going to play games with us or manipulate us. We sense this writer has become vulnerable enough to open up a vein and let us peek into his or her soul.

The problem with much "Christian writing" comes at this point. Those of us who write from a Christian perspective sometimes tend to be less than honest. When asked why religious poetry is often of such poor quality, T. S. Eliot said, "The capacity for writing poetry is rare; the capacity for religious emotion of the first intensity is rarer; and it is expected that the existence of both capacities in the same individual should be rarer still. People who write devotional verse are usually writing as they *want* to feel, rather than as they *do* feel" (quoted by Lockerbie, 49).

When we write what we want to feel instead of what we do feel, we come across as sincere but artificial. Perceptive readers can tell if we're opening up a vein or merely repeating pious clichés. This is what separates literary art from literary trivia. Literary art confronts us with the truth—even if we don't care to hear it. It is always written in somebody's blood.

A Simple Word

James Kilpatrick tells the story of a feature writer who was doing a piece on the United Fruit Company. He spoke of bananas once; he spoke of bananas twice; he spoke of bananas a third time, and then he was desperate. "The world's leading shippers of the elongated yellow fruit...," he wrote. Surely, a fourth banana would have been better (*The Writer's Art* [New York: Andrews, McNeel, & Parker, 1984) 38).

In the world of writing, there is a condition we might call "elongated yellow fruit syndrome." Writers afflicted with this condition want to impress people with long words and convoluted phrases. They seem to believe that such writing will convince readers of their intelligence.

A Congressional report on a bill intended to establish a national energy policy stated that the bill would give the president "a substantial measure of administrative flexibility to draft the price regulatory mechanism in a manner designed to optimize production from domestic properties subject to a statutory parameter requiring the regulatory pattern to prevent prices from exceeding a maximum weighted average" (Kilpatrick, 65).

What, I ask you, does that mean? The Congressional committee that produced that gobbledygook was in the advanced stages of "elongated yellow fruit syndrome." Haven't we all read books, heard sermons, or received office memos that went out of their way to be complicated and difficult? Haven't we all been victims (maybe even perpetrators) of "elongated yellow fruit syndrome"?

In his book *On Writing Well*, William Zinsser says writers should think of themselves as trail guides trying to tell people who are lost how to get out of the woods. If the directions are long and complicated, the lost searcher will quickly get frustrated and more confused. If the directions are simple and precise, the searcher will be grateful for the trail guide and eventually find his or her way home.

Thus, we have another way to spot literary art as opposed to literary trivia: literary art is so simple we can actually understand it and use it to find our way home.

A Creative Word

Nathan's story to David was truthful and simple, but it was also creative. He made parable out of a simple story so that David could be confronted by his own sin. His seemingly harmless story of a poor man's ewe lamb was actually a stick of dynamite powerful enough to explode David's hypocrisy.

Hundreds of years after Nathan told his tale, Jesus adopted the same strategy. He told truthful, simple parables that helped people discover significant truths. His stories were creative both because of their content and because of their style.

To say that the *content* of a written work is creative is to say that it teaches something new, or maybe that it teaches something old in a new way. Creative writing is fresh and comes from a person's deepest heart and deepest insight. When we read truly creative content, we know it. Through such writing, we can have an "aha!" moment that takes us to the truth.

To say that the *style* is creative is to say that the writing itself is fresh and alive. The writer has struggled to find just the right words to convey the truth. Mark Twain once said that the difference between the right word and the almost-right word is the difference between lightning and a lightning bug. A writer with creative style consistently gives us lightning, and we get "charged up" by that writer's way of stringing words together.

When we find a piece of writing that has both creative content and creative style, we have found an example of literary art. Those pieces are few and far between, but when we find them, we hug them to ourselves like long-lost friends. We have had a chance corroboration. We have sensed someone's spirit laid against ours. And in some way, large or small, we have had our lives changed by those words.

Conclusion

In her book *Bird by Bird*, Ann Lamott writes,

> Even if only the people in your writing group read your memoirs or stories or novel, even if you only wrote your story so that one day your children would know what life was like when you were a child and you knew the name of every dog in town— still to have written your version is an honorable thing to have done. Against all odds, you have put it down on paper, so that it won't be lost. And who knows? Maybe what you have written will help others, will be a small part of the solution. You don't even have to know how or in what way, but if you are writing the clearest, truest words you can find and doing the best you can to understand and communicate, this will shine on paper like its

own little lighthouse. Lighthouses don't go running all over an island looking for boats to save; they just stand there shining. (New York: Doubleday, 1994, pp. 235–36)

That's what good writers are: lighthouses who just stand there shining. And those of us who need direction and hope can run to those lighthouses for help. In the presence of literary art, we, like David, can see ourselves more clearly, change, and move ever closer to God. Honest, simple, creative words are some of God's best tools for growing our souls.

Notes

Notes

4

DRAMATIC ARTS

Ezekiel 37:15-28

Central Question

What can God teach me through drama and symbols?

Scripture

Ezekiel 37:15-28 15 The word of the LORD came to me: 16 Mortal, take a stick and write on it, "For Judah, and the Israelites associated with it"; then take another stick and write on it, "For Joseph (the stick of Ephraim) and all the house of Israel associated with it"; 17 and join them together into one stick, so that they may become one in your hand. 18 And when your people say to you, "Will you not show us what you mean by these?" 19 say to them, Thus says the LORD God: I am about to take the stick of Joseph (which is in the hand of Ephraim) and the tribes of Israel associated with it; and I will put the stick of Judah upon it, and make them one stick, in order that they may be one in my hand. 20 When the sticks on which you write are in your hand before their eyes, 21 then say to them, Thus says the Lord GOD: I will take the people of Israel from the nations among which they have gone, and will gather them from every quarter, and bring them to their own land. 22 I will make them one nation in the land, on the mountains of Israel; and one king shall be king over them all. Never again shall they be two nations, and never again shall they be divided into two kingdoms. 23 They shall never again defile themselves with their idols and their detestable things, or with any of their transgressions. I will save them from all the apostasies into which they have fallen, and will cleanse them. Then they shall be my people, and I will be their God. 24 My servant David shall be king over them; and they shall

all have one shepherd. They shall follow my ordinances and be careful to observe my statutes. 25 They shall live in the land that I gave to my servant Jacob, in which your ancestors lived; they and their children and their children's children shall live there forever; and my servant David shall be their prince forever. 26 I will make a covenant of peace with them; it shall be an everlasting covenant with them; and I will bless them and multiply them, and will set my sanctuary among them forevermore. 27 My dwelling place shall be with them; and I will be their God, and they shall be my people. 28 Then the nations shall know that I the LORD sanctify Israel, when my sanctuary is among them forevermore.

Reflecting

I had known about Communion all my life. The pastor was always solemn. The silver plates were passed from one pair of hands to another. The tiny little cups in the silver tray looked like amethysts in the morning light.

For a long time, the trays passed over me, from Mom to Dad. After I was baptized, I took a class and memorized verses on Communion (1 Cor 11:23-26). Then both plates passed through my hands long enough for me to partake, too. Years went by; the plates were passed once a quarter.

In high school, I saw the movie *Places in the Heart*, starring Sally Field and Danny Glover. The final scene shows a Communion service in a 1930s country church. Next to Sally Field's character sits her husband—a policeman who died earlier in the film. On her other side is the man who accidentally shot her husband in a drunken mistake.

At first glance, I was confused. Why was her dead husband there? Why was his killer there? What were they all doing in church together?

And then in hit me. *This was Communion*: all the saints, living and dead, together, all forgiven, all reunited. This is what we were doing "in remembrance of" Jesus every time we passed the bread and cup. In the few minutes it took to watch this scene, my theology widened and my sense of God deepened.

Sometimes God speaks to us through drama or symbols in a way that can rearrange our thinking. Today we look at God's use of drama through the prophet Ezekiel. This ancient scene invites us to explore how God uses drama to speak to us.

Studying

Ezekiel appreciated the power of drama because he had experienced it in his own life. He was a priest in Jerusalem, but the Babylonians forced him and Israel's other leaders and intellectuals into exile in 597 BC (Darr, 1075). In Babylon, God used a dramatic vision to call Ezekiel to be a prophet. His life as a prophet was defined by strange visions and unusual assignments from God. God directed him to do unusual acts like lying on his side for days on end and cutting off and burning his own hair. Scholars call these dramatic performances "sign-acts." They are teaching tools that involved acting out the point God was making (Darr, 1143).

In his early years as a prophet, Ezekiel preached judgment against the people's unfaithfulness to their covenant with God. He spoke out against worshiping other gods, dabbling in forbidden religious practices, and listening to false prophets (chs. 1–24). But after the

Other prophetic "sign-acts":
- Ahijah tears his mantle and gives ten of twelve pieces to Jeroboam (1 Kgs 11:29-39).
- Zedekiah fashions iron horns (1 Kgs 22:11).
- Elisha has King Joash shoot arrows or strike the ground with them (2 Kgs 13:14-19).
- Isaiah goes naked and barefoot for three years (Isa 20:3).
- Jeremiah hides and then retrieves a loincloth (Jer 13:1-11).
- Jeremiah carries a yoke around his neck (Jer 27–28).
- Ezekiel shuts himself up in his house (Ezek 3:22-27).
- Ezekiel "lays siege" to a miniature representation of Jerusalem (Ezek 4:1-3).
- Ezekiel lies first on his left side, then on his right (Ezek 4:4-8).
- Ezekiel eats bread cooked on human dung (Ezek 4:12-15).
- Ezekiel cuts his hair with a sword, burning some and scattering the rest (Ezek 5:1-3).
- Ezekiel portrays a person going into exile (Ezek 12:1-16).
- Zechariah fashions a crown and sets it on the head of the high priest (Zech 6:9-13).

Babylonians destroyed the temple and Jerusalem in 587 BC, the people were afraid God had completely abandoned them. Ezekiel responded with comfort and hope. His sign-acts focused on good news for the people. He relayed assurances that God had not forgotten them.

In our passage, God instructs Ezekiel to do another sign-act for the people. With God's temple ruined and their city destroyed, the people cannot imagine a hopeful future. But God gives Ezekiel a way to help them imagine God restoring what is lost and welcoming them home again. When everything has fallen apart, good news sometimes needs more than words to break through the desolation.

God tells Ezekiel to take two simple sticks and write on them. The first stick represents Judah, the southern kingdom, and all who live or once lived there. The second stick represents Israel's northern kingdom, called Israel, whose dominant tribe descended from Joseph's son Ephraim, and all who live or once lived there.

We recall that after Solomon's reign, the kingdom divided into two separate nations, Judah in the south with Jerusalem as its capital, and Israel in the north. First and Second Kings and 1–2 Chronicles tell this painful part of Israel's history, when the descendants of Jacob's twelve sons turned against each other. Jacob's descendants, already less powerful than their neighbors, became more vulnerable when they were divided.

> In the Bible, "Israel" sometimes refers to all the descendants of Jacob, north or south, and sometimes refers specifically to the northern kingdom with its capital at Samaria.

The two sticks symbolize Israel's broken past, current struggle, and shattered future. But God tells Ezekiel to "join them together into one stick so that they may become one in your hand" (v. 17). God does not explain how Ezekiel is to make the two sticks one. Either Ezekiel already knows how to do this or joining the sticks is God's job, not Ezekiel's. The focus is not on how he will do it but on how it will affect the people.

When the people ask what it means, God says to tell them, "I am about to...take the people of Israel from the nations among

which they have gone...and bring them to their own land"
(vv. 19, 21). This is God's promise that the scattered, demoralized
people of Israel will return home. It is good news: they will go
home to their historic promised land.

But that's not all! God says, "I will make them one nation in
the land...and one king shall be king over them all" (v. 22). They
are going home, and God will also unite them as one people
again—one nation under one king. God will heal the old divisions
and arguments that separated them, just as the two separate
sticks became one.

Under one king from David's line (vv. 24, 25), the people will
return to their covenant with God. God will "save them...and will
cleanse them" from past sins that separated them from God and
one another (v. 23). The king will guide them in following God's
commands (v. 24), enabling them and their offspring to live as
one in their homeland "forever" (v. 25). Never again will they face
exile or separation from God.

The one stick symbolizes "an everlasting covenant" that God
will make with them (v. 26). Echoing the promise to Abraham
(Gen 22:17), God says, "I will bless them and multiply them"
(v. 26). God ends by promising to dwell among them forever
(vv. 27-28). Though the temple has been destroyed and Jerusalem
is in ruins, God will restore Israel. Using two simple sticks, God
offers new life amid destruction.

Understanding

Sometimes when we are desolate, it is difficult to imagine a hopeful future. The weight of the present and all that has been lost is
simply too overpowering. Sometimes it is hard to imagine feeling
happy again, or even "normal."

The people of Israel felt abandoned by God. The exile was bad
enough; they were forced from home, away from the land God
had promised the people of Israel. They were cut off from the
temple and unable to participate in the religious festivals that
shaped their relationship with God. Prophets like Ezekiel challenged the people to consider how their own failure to live as

"priestly kingdom and a holy nation" (Exod 19:1-6) contributed to their exiled state.

And then things got worse. The Babylonians defeated Jerusalem and destroyed the temple Solomon had built, the place where God's presence dwelled—where even foreigners from "a distant land" would "hear of your great name, your mighty hand and your outstretched arm" (1 Kgs 8:42). With the temple destroyed and the holy city in ruins, was God still present with Israel? Were they stuck in Babylon forever?

God's image of two sticks becoming one sparks the people's collective imagination again. They had heard words of hope and comfort from Ezekiel. Now came an action, a symbol, that would jar their hope from its hiding place. The one stick representing the one people of Israel could be a touchstone for the people that they could remember in the days to come. God offered them a classic case of "seeing is believing."

The same is often true for us. Sometimes words may ring hollow. We need to see God's truth lived out before us, whether through a drama, movie scene, or symbol. God can use these different ways to say something new to us.

What About Me?

• *Consider times when God has used symbols to speak to or encourage you.* An artist friend of mine was recently commissioned by a hospital to make hundreds of etched stones for cancer patients. Each one bears a tiny spiral, like a finger labyrinth, and these words of Saint Julian of Norwich: "All shall be well." People can hold the stones during treatment or prayer, trace the tiny spirals, and trust that all shall be well with God, no matter the diagnosis. I think of these stones as literally "hope in hand." What symbols has God used to speak to you?

• *Movies and plays can be far more than entertainment.* Whether the director, producer, or actors intend it or not, most movies and plays can inform our faith. If we are thinking theologically, we can find themes of faith in any movie: sin (plenty of that!), loss, redemption, confession, transformation, reconciliation. A comedy can urge us to think about our relationships as well as make us laugh; an action flick can invite us to think about how God views "the bad guys." What movies or plays have spoken to you?

• *A faith and film group could be a great option for learning, growth, and community.* Most congregations have a movie buff or two. Watching a film (carefully chosen with the intended audience in mind) and reflecting on it with the help of a facilitator might be a good option for a small group, a Sunday school elective, or a short-term study. This could be a fun way to invite unchurched people to engage with believers. It could also deepen relationships within the church and across generations.

Resources

Kathryn Pfisterer Darr, "Ezekiel," *New Interpreter's Bible*, vol. 6 (Nashville: Abingdon, 2001).

James M. Efird, *The Old Testament Writings: History, Literature, Interpretation* (Atlanta: John Knox, 1982).

John Paterson, "Ezekiel," *The Old Testament and the Fine Arts*, ed. Cynthia P. Maus (New York: Harper and Brothers, 1954).

David L. Peterson, "Ezekiel: Introduction and Notes," *HarperCollins Study Bible* (New York: HarperCollins, 1993).

DRAMATIC ARTS

Ezekiel 35:15-28

Introduction

In the movie *Get Low* (Sony Pictures Classics, 2009), Robert
Duvall plays a hermit who has lived alone in the woods for years.
As the story develops we learn why he has retreated to his cabin
in the woods: he committed a terrible act as a young man and
never could get over it. The guilt and shame of his act made him
want to avoid people, so he moved to a cabin and kept to himself.
But his sin ate away at his soul and made him a miserable old
man. At the end of the movie, though, he is able to confess his act
publicly, find comfort in his confession, and reclaim his life.

My wife and I went to see this movie. As I left the theater, I
realized I had been "preached to" in the best sense of that phrase.
Quietly, the movie had snuck up on me and delivered a message
of sin, confession, and redemption. Many in the theater had
probably not been to church in a long time. Whether they realized it or not, they got a sermon when they watched *Get Low*. The
message was subtle but clear: anyone who has done something
wrong and feels ashamed can find forgiveness and reconciliation
through the simple but courageous act of confession. *Get Low*
delivers the same life-changing message as the parable of the
prodigal son.

That movie was a reminder to me of the power of drama. I
doubt many preachers in our country could have communicated
the message of sin, confession, and redemption as powerfully as
that movie did. As we have seen in the previous three lessons,
God can and does use visual arts, musical arts, and literary arts to
speak to us. Watching *Get Low* made me realize again that God
uses dramatic arts to speak to us, too.

A Play with a Happy Ending

Our passage tells us about a one-man play performed by the prophet Ezekiel. He sensed God telling him to act out a drama that would give people hope in the midst of a national tragedy.

First, Ezekiel took a stick and wrote on it, "For Judah, and the Israelites associated with it." Then he took a second stick and wrote on it, "For Joseph (the stick of Ephraim) and all the house of Israel associated with it." Finally, he joined the two sticks into one so that he could show the people one united stick. That one stick, Ezekiel went on to say, was a symbol of what God was going to do one day. God was going to unite Israel and Judah so that they would once again be one nation.

Perhaps a thumbnail sketch of Israel's history will help us understand the background of Ezekiel's object lesson. A simplified version of a long and complicated history looks like this:

• God calls Abram, promising to bless him and his descendants and to use them to bless the world.
• One of Abram's descendants, Joseph, is sold as a slave and carried to Egypt. Eventually, his entire family joins him there.
• The family grows through the years but is eventually enslaved. The family remains in slavery in Egypt until Moses arrives to liberate them.
• Led by Moses and then Joshua, the Israelites wander forty years in the wilderness before they finally arrive in the promised land of Canaan.
• Once in Canaan, the Israelites are oppressed by a succession of foreign peoples and start to long for a king who will deliver them and unite them as a nation.
• After a false start with Saul, David eventually becomes that longed-for king. A mere two generations after David's death, though, the nation of Israel has been split into two nations— Israel in the north and Judah in the south.
• Two centuries after that (about 722 BC), Israel is overrun by the Assyrians, and the people are forcibly evacuated.
• Judah struggles on, focused on Jerusalem, its center of both wealth and worship. But in 587 BC, the southern kingdom is conquered by the Babylonian Empire. Jerusalem is ransacked, the

temple is destroyed, and many of the people of Judah are hauled off to Babylon.

It was at this dark time in Israel's history that Ezekiel wrote his prophecy and enacted the one-man play we're studying this week. In that dark, desolate time, his play had a happy ending. He gave the disillusioned people an image of the Israelites reuniting under a new king: "I will make them one nation in the land, on the mountains of Israel; and one king shall be king over them all. Never again shall they be two nations, and never again shall they be divided into two kingdoms" (Ezek 37:22).

He also gave them an image of God blessing them and giving them peace: "I will make a covenant of peace with them; it shall be an everlasting covenant with them; and I will bless them and multiply them, and will set my sanctuary among them forevermore" (Ezek 37:26).

About fifty years later, the Persian Empire conquered the Babylonians and allowed the people of Judah to go back home. The ten lost tribes of Israel, deported earlier by the Assyrians, never made it home, but at least the people of Judah did. Ezekiel's message of hope wasn't just wishful thinking. The people did get to go home, rebuild the temple, reestablish their relationship with God, and be a restored nation.

To people devastated by the Babylonian invasion, Ezekiel's drama about the two sticks was a symbol of hope. Days of unity were coming. Days of peace and God's blessing were on the horizon. His simple object lesson was actually a powerful sermon about trusting the sovereignty of God.

Catching the Truth

One reason drama is so effective is that it doesn't hit us over the head with truth. Rather, it presents us with a story and lets us draw our own conclusions from it. For most people, catching the truth is much more enjoyable and effective than being hit over the head by it.

The philosopher Søren Kierkegaard wrote much about the Christian culture of his native Denmark. He was convinced that indirect communication of the gospel would be more effective in

Denmark than direct communication. He likened most Christian communication he heard to a man sawing a board and pressing too hard on the saw. To cut the board effectively, he needed to lighten up and use a softer touch. So too, Kierkegaard said, most Christian communicators pushed too hard, and in the process they drove people away. Kierkegaard called for preachers to lighten up and use a softer touch to reach people with the gospel.

That's precisely why drama is so effective. It tells us a story, but it never hits us head-on and never spells out truths for us. When we watch a play, movie, or television program, we either "get" its truths or we don't, but the burden is on us. We have to discern what truth (if any) is in the story.

It has taken me years to learn that hitting people over the head with truth is not the purpose of a sermon. Far more times than I care to mention, I have preached sermons in which I (1) told the congregation what I was going to say, (2) said what I was going to say, and (3) repeated what I had just said in my conclusion. Then, just in case there was some real slacker in the crowd who hadn't been listening, I repeated my message in the prayer at the end of the sermon. Those sermons were like being hit by a sledgehammer—not once but four times!

I now think Ezekiel's way is better. Hold up a stick and talk briefly about it. I now think a movie like *Get Low* communicates more powerfully than most sermons for the same reason. It tells a story and lets the viewers draw their own conclusions. Drama *shows*; it doesn't tell. There's something about respecting people enough to let them make up their own minds that is always winsome and persuasive.

Drama at Church

Why don't we use drama more often and more effectively at church? I think there are two reasons—one bad and one good.

The bad reason we don't use drama in the church is we don't trust drama to convey the truth. Schooled in the old "hit them over the head" method of communication, we think drama is too indirect and open-ended. The church trusts direct communication much more than indirect communication. Therefore, it gives the impression that it can't trust the worshipers to discern the truth. If we haven't hit them with a sledgehammer—and most drama doesn't—we think we haven't really preached the gospel.

The good reason we don't use drama in the church is we know that drama, to be effective, must be done well. A poorly rehearsed skit in the worship service is likely to be a disaster. A first-person sermon by the pastor in his bathrobe is probably going to be laughable. Trying to do a full-fledged dramatic production with a cast of church members is almost guaranteed to be second-rate. Because we can't do drama well, we often don't do it at all.

But surely there are legitimate ways to bring drama into the church sanctuary. Our church has tried several ways of using drama in our services. We've had youth read the Scripture antiphonally, and it has brought meaning and depth to that part of our worship service. We've had several productions of plays, like *The Cotton Patch Gospel*, that were performed in our sanctuary, using some professional actors and some of our church members. We recently asked a professional actress to do a one-act play and invited the public to attend performances at our church. We've talked about having a summertime music-and-drama workshop for kids and letting them put on a show at the end of their week together.

The opportunities are limitless once we become convinced of the power of drama to convey truth and change lives. In a world where people are sick of sledgehammers, drama holds great potential for declaring God's love.

Conclusion

In his book *Simply Christian*, N. T. Wright says,

> [T]he church should reawaken its hunger for beauty at every level. This is essential and urgent. It is essential to Christian living that we should celebrate the goodness of creation, ponder its present brokenness, and, insofar as we can, celebrate in advance the healing of the world, the new creation itself. Art, music, literature, dance, theater, and many other expressions of human delight and wisdom, can all be explored in new ways. (New York: HarperOne, 2006, p. 235)

During this unit of study, we have looked at ways we can explore the arts in our individual lives and in our churches— through visual arts, musical arts, literary arts, and dramatic arts. The arts open up new ways for us to experience God, and we dare not miss those opportunities.

Wright goes on to say, "The arts are not the pretty but irrelevant bits around the border of reality. They are highways into the center of a reality which cannot be glimpsed, let alone grasped, any other way" (235).

Just as surely as God speaks through Scripture, sermons, and Sunday school lessons, God speaks through paintings, songs, books, and movies. It would be sad to think that in overlooking the arts, we missed out on experiencing a big part of God.

Notes

Notes

Other available titles from

NextSunday
Resources

1 Peter
Keep Hope Alive

This study of First Peter focuses on keeping hope alive in the face of pressures and circumstances that could possibly extinguish it completely, or worse, turn authentic faith into a pale replica of the real thing.

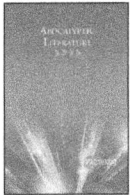

Apocalyptic Literature

This study examines five apocalyptic texts in the Bible—from Zechariah, Daniel, Matthew, and Revelation. With each new year bringing a new prediction of impending doom, it is always a perfect time to get the story straight. Apocalyptic literature does not address the future. It addresses our present.

Approaching a Missional Mindset

The World isn't the same as it once was. We must be the church in a new place, in unimagined ways, and with a wider range of people. Engage your small group with the radical and refreshing challenge of developing a "missional lifestyle."

Baptist Freedom
Celebrating Our Baptist Heritage

What makes a Baptist a Baptist? Of course, the ultimate answer is simple: membership in a local Baptist church. But there are all kinds of Baptist churches! What are the spiritual and theological marks of a Baptist? What is the shape and the feel of Baptist Christianity?

Challenges of the Christian Life

The way of the cross is difficult, and taking Jesus seriously means looking honestly at how we fall short of God's best hopes for us and seeing how much we need God's grace. For all of us there are times when we need to remember that Christ is our saving grace and recommit ourselves to the journey of faith, rediscovering, again and again, the life-giving purpose described in the book of Ephesians.

Christ Is Born!

Even in the midst of difficult circumstances, Advent is a time when we can find hope. Much like today, people in the 1st century church faced struggles. Examining the Gospel of Matthew, lessons covered are "Waiting for Christ," "Preparing for Christ," "Expecting Christ," "Announcing Christ," and "The Arrival of Christ."

Christmas in Mark

In the early chapters of Mark, we will encounter a Christmas story. This story, however, will not be quite like the one told by other Gospel writers, but it will resonate with the reality of your life. Mark doesn't deny the beauty or reality of the nativity; however, he seems to believe that Christmas begins—the gospel begins—when Christ intrudes upon the hard realities of life.

Christians and Hunger

These sessions challenge us to apply gospel lenses and holy imagination to what literally gives us energy to live: food. With God's grace, we have the opportunity to imagine communities where tables are large and all are fed.

The Church on a Mission

What does it mean to be a church on a mission? The lesson of Acts 1:8 is that we must simultaneously carry out Christ's mandate at home, in our region, in places that have been our blind spots, and around the world.

Colossians
Living the Faith Faithfully
Paul's letter to the Colossians begins with a high-minded philosophical defense of the faith, but concludes with a collection of extremely practical advice for living by faith. This study addresses the questions many Christians face today, helping them apply Paul's practical advice in their own lives.

Easter Confessions
Easter confession is often found on many different lips in the Gospel of John. When we listen carefully, those ancient confessions still echo into this new millennium.

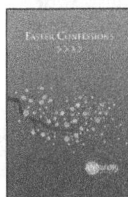

Embracing the Word of God
We live during a time of transition in Christian history. Basic assumptions about the truth of the Christian faith are being questioned, not only by nonbelievers, but by Christians themselves. First John offers a starting point for understanding of what it means to "be" Christian.

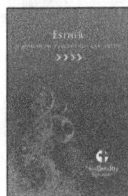

Esther: A Woman of Discretion and Valor
The book of Esther is not a record of historical facts as such. Rather, it is a magnificent narrative that refuses to interpret life as being driven by coincidence or happenstance. In the otherwise unknown characters of Esther, Haman, and Mordecai, we trace the movement of the divine hand as God collaborates with God's risk-taking people to rescue them from the hand of their enemies.

Facing Life's Challenges
This study explores four significant challenges common to most persons of faith: the challenge of new light, the challenge of time's limit, the challenge of living with mystery, and the challenge of authentic spirituality. Although these issues are neither simple nor easy to ponder, this study effectively leads us in confronting these challenges.

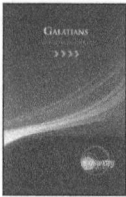

Galatians
Freedom in Christ

Paul wrote with fiery passion, as you will notice from the opening paragraphs of this letter to the Galatians. But his language reveals that he was writing about a crucially important issue—the very nature of salvation in Christ.

How Does the Church Decide?

An array of decisions draw energy and time from church members. These decisions may be theological, such as mode of baptism, aesthetic, such as the color of the sanctuary carpet, or functional, such as the selection of a new minister. This study will consider how the church has made its decisions in the past to help guide our decisions today.

A Holy and Surprising Birth

Christmas begins here—discover these five love stories and renew your appreciation of God's laborious effort to birth our salvation.

Is God Calling?

Witness the varying forms of God's call, the variety of people called, and the variety of responses. Perhaps God's call to you will become clearer.

James
Gaining True Wisdom

If we'll be honest with God and ourselves as we study what James says, we can make great strides toward wisdom and a living faith.

Life Lessons from Bathsheba

Who was Bathsheba? She was a complex figure who developed from the silent object of David's lust into a powerful, vocal, and influential queen mother.

Life Lessons from David

In the Bible, we catch David in the various stages of the human journey: childhood, adolescence, adulthood, and senior adulthood. From the biblical treatment of the stages of David's life, we can land some insights to assist us in better understanding the human journey.

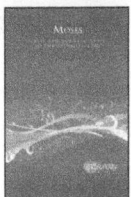

Moses
From the Burning Bush to the Promised Land

We would do well to trace the life of Moses so we might discover how his life changed, both personally and as Israel's leader, as he learned what it meant to love God with all his heart, soul, and strength.

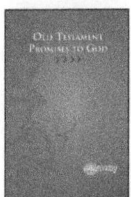

Old Testament Promises to God

Some individuals may feel that our promises couldn't possibly mean anything to God. Perhaps the real question is this: under what circumstances should or do we make such promises? The Old Testament contains several examples of people making promises to God, using the unique form of a biblical "vow."

The Prayer Life of Jesus

The study of Jesus' prayer life can deepen our own prayer practices. These five sessions examine the importance of prayer at various stages of Jesus' life and ministry. He made no important decisions without consulting God.

Proverbs for Living

Long ago, a collection of wise teachers committed themselves to the ways of God and collect this wisdom into what we know as the book of Proverbs. These four lessons explore the simple truth of Proverbs: There is a good life to be had—a life lived in faithfulness to God.

Seeking Holiness in the Sermon on the Mount

The Sermon on the Mount has long been recognized as the pinnacle of Jesus' teaching. But with this importance in mind, it's easy to think of Jesus' teachings as lofty and idealistic, offering little guidance for everyday life. Perhaps Jesus' sermon allows us to see beyond ourselves, beyond our own failures and shortcomings—revealing God's intention for our lives.

Spiritual Disciplines
Obligation or Opportunity?

The spiritual disciplines help deepen a believer's faith and increases his or her intimacy with Christ. In this study, we take a deeper look at some of the disciplines and consider their practice as a response to God's love.

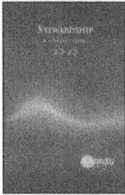

Stewardship
A Way of Living

Great News! Stewardship is not about money! At least not *just* about money. Certainly, stewardship relates to money, and, yes, we need to tithe. However, stewardship branches out into multiple areas of life. Properly practiced, this act of service can lead to peace and purpose in living.

The Ten Commandments

When the Ten Commandments are in the news, it is usually because a judge or teacher has hung them up on the walls. The Ten Commandments do not need to be posted or even preached nearly so much as they need to be practiced and viewed as life-giving, joyful affirmations of a better way of life.

www.ingramcontent.com/pod-product-compliance
Lightning Source LLC
Chambersburg PA
CBHW060702030426
42337CB00017B/2723